The Wild World of Animals

Bears

Paws, Claws, and Jaws

by Adele D. Richardson

Consultant:
Kimberley S. McGrath
Executive Director
The American Bear Association

Bridgestone Books
an imprint of Capstone Press
Mankato, Minnesota

Bridgestone Books are published by Capstone Press
151 Good Counsel Drive, P.O. Box 669, Mankato, Minnesota 56002
http://www.capstone-press.com

Library of Congress Cataloging-in-Publication Data
Richardson, Adele, 1966–
     Bears: paws, claws, and jaws/by Adele D. Richardson.
     p. cm.—(The wild world of animals)
     Includes bibliographical references (p. 24) and index.
     ISBN 0-7368-0823-X
     1. Bears—Juvenile literature. [1. Bears.] I. Title. II. Series.
QL737.C27 R52 2001
599.78—dc21
                                                                00-010264

Summary: A simple introduction to bears describing their physical characteristics, habitat,
young, food, enemies, and relationship to people.

Editorial Credits
Sarah Lynn Schuette, editor; Karen Risch, product planning editor; Linda Clavel,
     designer and illustrator; Kimberly Danger and Heidi Schoof, photo researchers

Photo Credits
GeoIMAGERY/Robert Winslow, 4; Lindsey P. Martin, 8, 18; Neil Evans, 10
PhotoDisc, Inc., cover, 1, 6, 16
Photo Network/Howard Folsom, 12
Unicorn Stock Photos/Robert VanKirk, 20
Visuals Unlimited/Milton Tierney, Jr., 14

1 2 3 4 5 6 06 05 04 03 02 01

Table of Contents

brown bear

jaw

claws

paws

Bears

Bears can be large or small. All bears have large paws, sharp claws, and strong jaws. They have short tails and legs. Bears can have black, brown, or cream fur. They have round heads and small ears.

American black bear

FUN FACTS

Eight kinds of bears live in the world. There are brown bears, American black bears, Asian black bears, polar bears, giant pandas, sun bears, sloth bears, and spectacled bears.

Bears Are Mammals

Bears and other mammals are warm-blooded and have a backbone. Female mammals give birth to live young that drink milk from their mothers. Bears can swim, run, and climb trees like many other mammals.

warm-blooded

having a body temperature that stays the same

polar bear

A Bear's Habitat

Bears live in habitats around the world. Polar bears often walk on cold arctic ice. Black bears and sun bears live in forests. Brown bears sometimes wander near mountain streams. Panda bears live in the bamboo forests of China.

habitat

the place where
an animal lives

panda bear

FUN FACTS

Some panda bears spend up to 16 hours per day eating bamboo. Bamboo is a plant with a hard, hollow stem. This plant only grows in China.

What Do Bears Eat?

Bears eat both plants and animals. Panda bears chew bamboo. Polar bears eat seals and walruses. Sloth bears have long tongues to scoop up termites. Some bears use their claws to dig for grubs. Black bears and brown bears catch fish with their jaws and claws.

termite
an insect that looks like an ant

brown bear

Hunting for Food

Bears are excellent hunters. They use their good sense of smell to find animals and plants to eat. Sometimes they run quickly to catch prey. Bears also dive underwater to catch fish in streams and rivers.

prey

an animal hunted by another animal for food

spectacled bear mother and cub

Bear Parents

Many adult bears live alone. Male and female bears come together to mate during the spring and summer. Female bears give birth to bear cubs in the winter. They have one to five cubs in a litter.

litter

a group of animals born at the same time

brown bear cub

FUN FACTS

A group of bears is a sloth. Male bears are boars. Female bears are sows.

Bear Cubs

Bear cubs are very small at birth. They sometimes weigh less than 1 pound (.5 kilograms). They are blind and have little fur. Cubs grow quickly. Mother bears take care of their cubs for one to two years.

polar bear

Hibernation

Some bears hibernate in dens during winter. A den can be a cave or a pile of leaves. Some bears dig dens in the ground with their claws. Polar bears dig holes in the snow. Cubs are usually born in dens.

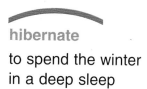

hibernate

to spend the winter in a deep sleep

sun bear

FUN FACTS

The sun bear is often called "honey bear." Many bears eat honey from bee hives. A bear's thick fur coat protects it from bee stings.

Protecting Bears

Many people work to protect bears and their habitats. Some people teach classes about bears and how they live. They also show people how to stay safe around bears. You can help keep bears' habitat clean and safe by not throwing garbage on the ground.

Hands On: Keeping Warm

Polar bears have black skin under their fur. This black skin helps keep polar bears warm. You can see how black surfaces soak up the sun's heat.

What You Need

A sunny day
1 piece of white paper
1 piece of black paper
A large baking sheet
2 rocks
A watch or a clock

What You Do

1. Find a sunny place outside.
2. Put the pieces of white and black paper side-by-side on the baking sheet. Put a rock on each sheet of paper to hold it down.
3. Leave the baking sheet in the sun for 15 minutes.
4. Feel each piece of paper.

The side with the black paper is much warmer. Dark colors soak up the sun's heat. The sun's heat bounces off light colors. A polar bear's black skin soaks up the sun's heat to keep the bear warm.

Words to Know

bamboo (bam-BOO)—a plant with a hard, hollow stem; panda bears eat bamboo.

den (DEN)—an animal's home; bear cubs usually are born in dens.

grub (GRUHB)—an insect that looks like a short, white worm

hibernate (HYE-bur-nate)—to spend the winter in a deep sleep; some bears hibernate in dens during the winter.

litter (LIT-ur)—a group of animals born to one mother at one time; female bears often give birth to a litter of two cubs.

mate (MATE)—to join together to produce young; bears mate during spring and summer.

termite (TUR-mite)—an insect that looks like an ant; termites live in mounds of dirt.

Read More

Berger, Melvin. *Growl! A Book About Bears.* Hello Reader!
New York: Scholastic, 1999.
Holmes, Kevin J. *Bears.* Animals. Mankato, Minn.:
Bridgestone Books, 1998.

Internet Sites

The Bear Den-Species By Species
http://www.bearden.org/species.html
The Cub Den
http://www.nature-net.com/bears/cubden.html
Defenders of Wildlife-Kids' Planet
http://www.kidsplanet.org

Index